HOW THEY LIVED

A MEDIEVAL SERF

STEWART ROSS

Illustrated by
Alan Langford

HOW THEY LIVED

A Family in World War II
A Medieval Serf
A Roman Centurion
A Victorian Factory Worker

First published in 1985 by
Wayland (Publishers) Limited
49 Lansdowne Place, Hove,
East Sussex, BN3 1HF, England

ISBN 0 85078 500 6

Typeset by Planagraphic Typesetters Limited
Printed in Italy by G. Canale & C.S.p.A., Turin
Bound in the UK by The Pitman Press

CONTENTS

A TOUGH LIFE   4

A MEDIEVAL VILLAGE   6

A SERF'S HOUSE   8

FAMILY LIFE   10

THE OPEN FIELDS   12

SERFS AT WORK   14

WHAT SERFS WORE   16

FOOD AND DRINK   18

HEALTH AND SICKNESS   20

LANGUAGE   22

GOING TO CHURCH   24

HOLIDAYS AND SPORTS   26

WAR AND REBELLION   28

THE END OF SERFDOM   30

GLOSSARY   31

MORE BOOKS TO READ   31

INDEX   32

A TOUGH LIFE

It was a freezing morning. Thick ice covered the village pond, and chickens fluffed out their feathers for warmth. In a small hut a man woke up. He pulled on woollen stockings, grabbed a piece of dried meat, and went to the door.

The man swore when he felt the cold air. Wrapping his cloak more closely round his thin shoulders, he trudged towards the distant fields. He had a ditch to dig, not on his own land, but on his lord's. The man was a serf, and a serf's life was very tough.

There were serfs in England in the early Middle Ages. During this time only about 2½ million people lived in

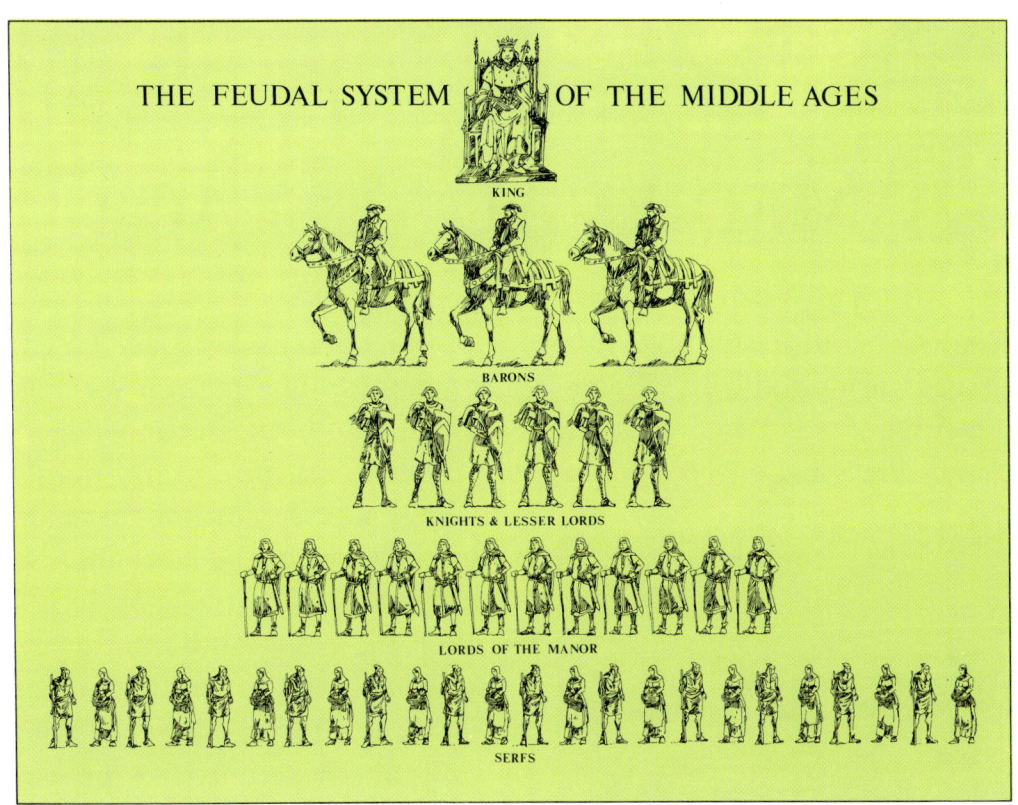

THE FEUDAL SYSTEM OF THE MIDDLE AGES

KING

BARONS

KNIGHTS & LESSER LORDS

LORDS OF THE MANOR

SERFS

England. Most of them lived in small villages in the country. Life was simple and hard: there was not even electricity or tap water.

The king owned most of the land. He gave huge estates to his barons, who had to serve him. The barons gave land to lesser lords and knights. The serfs were at the bottom of this arrangement. They farmed land which belonged to their local lord. This organization is called the feudal system. You can see a diagram of it on this page.

A Medieval Village

The English countryside of the Middle Ages was dotted with villages. At the centre of each one was the church and the village green. This

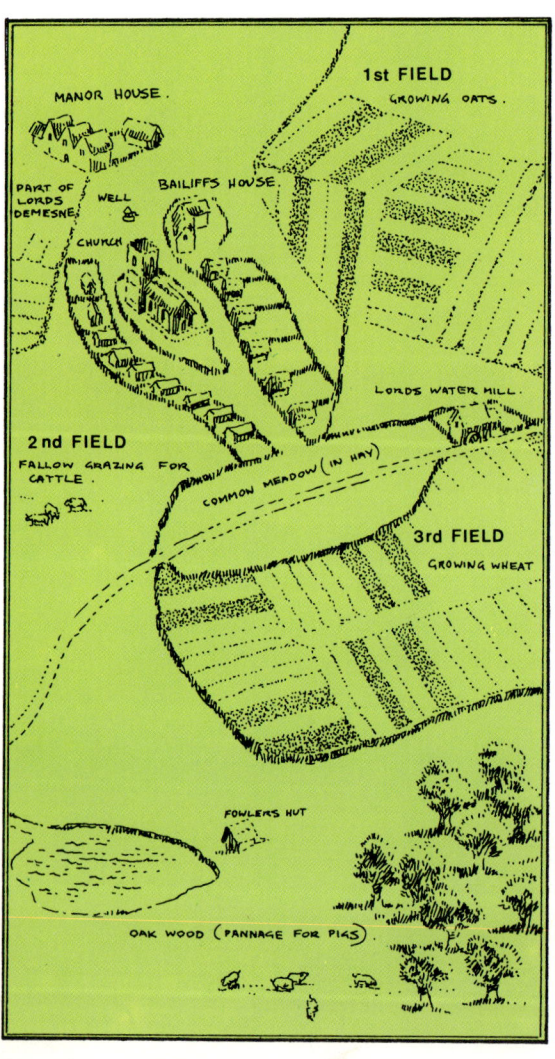

was an open grassy space for meetings or games. The church was easily the biggest building in the village.

The most important man in the village was the lord of the manor. He owned most of the land and lived in a large manor house. The serfs had to obey his commands, or he wouldn't let them use the land.

Many villages were very small, with only about seventy-five people living in them. The big villages, of perhaps 150 families, had everything they needed. They had their own black-smiths, carpenters, brewers, and perhaps even their own shoemakers.

All villages had to have a mill, where the corn could be ground to make flour for bread. Around some villages were small fields, like there are today. But usually in the Middle Ages most of the land was divided into three or four huge fields. Each field was at least as big as two hundred football pitches!

Left *Most villages in the Middle Ages were surrounded by three or four huge fields.*

There was also plenty of common land. This was shared by everybody, and used for grazing pigs and cows. Most people spent all their lives in the same village. People knew each other very well and always knew what everyone else was up to!

Above *All villages had a mill, in which corn was ground.*

When the lord and lady rode through the village the serfs had to stand back to let them pass.

A Serf's House

Medieval serfs lived in little cottages, each with a garden around it. These cottages usually had two rooms — one for people and one for animals. The insides of the cottages were dark, dirty and probably smelly.

In the north of England the serfs built strong stone houses, but in the south or midlands, cottages had walls of mud and sticks. The roofs were made of thatch, with no chimneys.

Windows were just holes in the walls with shutters. There was no glass. A fortunate serf might have a cruck house. This was made by cutting two trees in half. Two halves made an arch, and a pole was put along the top of the arches.

Serfs' cottages were only about five metres square. All the family lived in the one room. A fire for cooking and heating burned on the earth floor.

Poor people lived in very small houses in the Middle Ages. Most homes had only one room with a fire burning in the middle.

Above *A serf's house often had no windows and only a very simple door.*

Smoke filled the air, so that the ceiling might have soot on it three centimetres thick!

The family slept on bundles of straw on the floor. Sometimes they used logs as pillows. There were no lavatories or washing places. The cottages were so small and simple that they could be moved easily. In 1426 a man called William Found ran away from his village, carrying his cottage with him!

The lords of the manor lived in much grander houses.

FAMILY LIFE

In medieval times, weddings took place at the church door.

Normally serfs didn't marry for love. Marriages were arranged by parents. Children were often not wanted because they were expensive to feed. It was several years before they could help in the home or fields.

Serfs married when they were quite old. This was because they had to have the lord of the manor's permission, and he would make them pay up to half a year's wages. Weddings took place at the church door. There was much excitement, but the serfs couldn't afford to buy special clothes to wear.

Babies were usually only given a Christian name at their baptism.

Women had many children. They were born at home, on the floor of the cottage. In these dirty conditions most babies died before they were three. Often their mothers died too. There were no doctors or hospitals to look after the sick. Babies were baptised in church as soon as possible. An old saying went: 'A child before he is baptised is not a child of God but a child of the Devil'.

Today most men and women live to over 70. In medieval times the average life was about 30 years. A serf of 40 was an old man. There was a funeral almost every week in the village. People were used to death, and no one was too sad when a coffin passed on its way to the village churchyard.

THE OPEN FIELDS

The three or four big village fields were divided into strips. Each strip was about 22 yards (20 metres) wide, and 220 yards (200 metres) long. This length was a furrow-long, now called a furlong.

A serf had several strips in different fields. Every year one field was left fallow, or bare. In the second field rye or wheat was sown in the winter. Oats or barley was sown in the spring in the other field. The crops were moved round each year.

Here is the work that the serfs did on their own land during the year:

All farm work was done by hand.

Winter — Sowing wheat or rye. Seed was sown by scattering it by hand. This was called broadcasting. Digging ditches, mending fences or hedges.

Spring — Sowing oats or barley. Harrowing. Weeding.

Summer — Weeding. Haymaking. Harvesting. Sickles were used to cut the hay and corn. After it had been carried home, corn was thrashed and winnowed. This separated the straw and chaff from the corn itself.

Autumn — Ploughing. The serfs shared their ploughs, and the oxen that pulled them.

Farmers prayed for good harvests. Some years the serfs had spare corn, which they could sell, but in lean years they starved.

This picture shows the work that serfs did at different times of the year.

SERFS AT WORK

A serf was not free to do what he wanted. He always had to farm his lord's land before his own. He had to grind his corn in his lord's mill. He even had to get his lord's permission to plough an extra piece of land. The lord of the manor's farm was called the demesne. A serf had to work on the demesne for two to three days each week. The lord had a bailiff, who made sure that the serfs did their work properly.

All the family who were old enough helped with the work. Women made ale and bread, and looked after the

These serfs are threshing the corn to remove the chaff from the grain, which is then carried away in baskets.

chickens, goats and cows. There were no schools in medieval villages. Children watched over the sheep and pigs on the common land. They also tried to catch fish or birds to eat.

Everyone helped in the fields at harvest time. The men cut the corn. The women and children tied it in bundles, called sheaves. This was hard work, and it lasted all the long hours of daylight.

Above *Trees were felled in autumn and winter.*

Below *Milk from cows and goats was used to make butter and cheese.*

In the winter life was very different. The poor could not afford candles. They had to stay indoors, huddled around their fires, from sunset to sunrise. In December, the darkness lasted for up to sixteen hours.

WHAT SERFS WORE

In you look carefully at the pictures on these pages, you can seen what serfs wore. Serfs had little or no money, so their clothes were very simple, and they had very few.

Men wore a long woolly shirt, called a kirtle, which came down to their knees. Underneath, they might have a linen shirt. In the winter they wrapped scarves round their heads.

A serf's clothes were few and simple.

Women wore long gowns which came down to the ground. Under the gown they might wear a shirt. All women covered their heads with hoods.

A serf probably had a leather jacket for the winter. His wife might have a pretty belt for her best gown. But their clothes were not often washed, and they had no special underclothes. A serf and his family slept in their dirty kirtles and gowns.

Above *It must have been difficult to work wearing long gowns like these.*

Left *A medieval leather boot.*

Men and women wore wool stockings. Shoes were made of leather or wood. In 1350 a pair of leather shoes cost six pence. This was expensive for a serf. A shepherd could only earn ten pence a month! When he needed money, a serf had to sell some food or wool, or send his wife and children out to work.

FOOD AND DRINK

Medieval serfs were very thin, because they often didn't have enough food. They normally ate only what they produced themselves. If the harvest was good, there was plenty of dark, rough bread. Peas, beans and onions were grown in the garden. A serf might have a cow, or share one with another family. This gave milk, from which cheese was made. Chickens scratching about the cottage produced eggs. Many families also kept pigs or sheep on the common. So a serf would quite often have meat to eat.

At harvest time, the serfs took their food and drink to the fields with them.

Above *Meat was often roasted over a spit.*

Most food was cooked in a big iron pot hung over the open fire. 'Pottage' was a popular vegetable stew. Meat could be roasted on a spit. The serf and his family had only two meals a day. Dinner was in the middle of the morning, and supper was at about 4 o'clock in the afternoon. How often they must have gone to bed hungry, especially on cold winter evenings!

Above *A medieval storage jar.*

There were no forks or spoons. The serf ate off wooden plates with a knife and his fingers. Mugs were made of leather. It is said that a woman once cut a piece off her shoe to patch a leaking mug! The family drank water and milk, but usually for dinner and supper they had cider or thick, sweet ale.

19

HEALTH AND SICKNESS

In medieval times people knew very little about medicine. They did not understand about dirt and germs. Serfs might swim in lakes or rivers, but they never took baths. Their bodies were crawling with lice and fleas.

If a serf broke an arm or leg, he was lucky if it healed straight. Cuts often went septic. Many people went blind, and food poisoning was frequent. But men and women were tougher in those days. They could eat food which would make us very ill.

Cures for diseases often did more harm than good. Leeches were put on patients to suck their blood. A hot plaster of honey and pigeon's dung was recommended as a treatment for bad kidneys.

Every now and again a serious disease, like typhoid, would sweep through the village, killing many people. The worst plague came in 1348-9. This was called the Black Death. Almost half the people in England were killed by this horrible disease. Men and women felt pains in

the chest, and they were sick. Black lumps came up on their bodies. They died in three days. In the village of Sladen in Buckinghamshire not a single person survived.

Left *Medical treatment was very primitive in the Middle Ages.*

Below *The Black Death reduced the English population from four million to about two million.*

LANGUAGE

In early medieval England the serfs spoke a language called Anglo-Saxon. The king and his barons spoke French. Slowly French and Anglo-Saxon mixed together. By 1400 all people were speaking a language like the English we use.

We get many of our country words from the Anglo-Saxon of the serfs. They talked about 'sheep'. The lords, speaking French, used the word 'mutton'. Both these words are now used in English.

Here is the first line of a poem called *Piers the Plowman*. John Langland wrote it in 1362. Can you understand it?

In a somer seson, whan soft was the sonne.

Words like 'soft', 'in', 'was' and 'the' are the same as we use today. 'Plowman' is easy to understand too.

Try saying the words 'whan', 'somer' and 'sonne' out loud. Can you

During the early Middle Ages, the king and his barons spoke French while the serfs spoke Anglo-Saxon.

guess what they mean? 'Whan' is when, 'somer' is summer, and 'sonne' is sun. The word 'seson' is a little more difficult. It means season.

So, in our language, the poet is saying:

In the summer season, when the sun was soft.

Langland wrote poetry towards the end of the Middle Ages. But he does give us an idea how men and women spoke six or seven hundred years ago.

Right *The printing press was not invented until the fifteenth century. Before then, books were written by hand, often by monks, and beautifully decorated. You can see part of one in the picture* **below.**

GOING TO CHURCH

The church was usually the only stone building in the village. Medieval churches were very strong. The serfs sometimes used them as castles when their villages were being attacked by

Below *A picture of Mary and baby Jesus from a medieval manuscript.*

Above *A bellringer summons the serfs to church for Sunday mass.*

Religion was very important to the serf. He was christened and married in church. He was buried in the churchyard, with a funeral service. He was supposed to go to church at least once a week.

Serfs had no education and they did not understand science. Religion helped them to explain things. For example, they thought that the Black Death was a punishment from God.

enemies. Inside, the walls of the churches were covered with pictures of Bible stories, to help the serfs learn about Christianity. They couldn't read the Bible for themselves.

Each village had a priest. He was the second most important man in the village, after the lord of the manor. Priests could read and write Latin. This was the language in which the church services were held. The serfs couldn't understand the services at

Above *Some medieval churches are still standing to this day. This is Shelsley Walsh church in England.*

all. They thought that they were some sort of magic.

The serfs had to give one-tenth of everything they produced to the priest. In hard times this made them very angry. In 1381 they were so furious that they rebelled, and cut off the Archbishop of Canterbury's head.

HOLIDAYS AND SPORTS

A serf's life was hard, but he did have some fun. In each village there was an ale house. Men and women met there, as they do in a pub today, to drink and gossip.

No one in the Middle Ages had long holidays. Instead, on Sundays and holy days, people had to stop work. The word holiday comes from holy day. On these festivals villagers danced on the green, to music played on a pipe and drum. There was much drinking and rowdy behaviour.

The sport at which the English were best was archery. It is said that a man called William Cloudesle could hit a staff at 400 metres. Men also played rough football matches. Sometimes they took place between two whole villages. They were like a friendly fight, with no rules. In 1314 King Edward II banned football because it caused so many riots.

The best holidays were May Day, Christmas Day and Midsummer's Day. The serfs forgot their dull lives, and went wild with delight. Acrobats and jugglers visited the big villages, and sometimes actors stopped to perform simple plays. The most cruel sport was bear-baiting. A bear was tied to a post, and dogs were set to attack it. At first the bear drove them away, but when it was exhausted the dogs killed it with their teeth.

Some one penny coins from medieval times.

Below *Feast days gave the serfs a chance to enjoy themselves and spend what little money they had.*

WAR AND REBELLION

Every serf had to fight for his lord if he was needed. This was part of their feudal duty. But serfs did not make good soldiers. They were not well trained, and they often went home in August to help with the harvest.

Because of the feudal system there were many different lords and barons who were often jealous of each other. So serfs were used to fighting. They had their own knives, bows and arrows. Sometimes they joined together and fought against their lords, instead

of fighting with them. This was called a rebellion.

Some rebels ran away into the huge forests that covered England. They became outlaws. Anyone could kill them, and claim a reward. The most famous outlaw was Robin Hood, of Sherwood Forest, near Nottingham. According to the legends, he attacked the cruel lords and rich priests.

The most famous rebellion took place in 1381. Thousands of poor people gathered together, and marched to London. They burned many manor houses and killed the lords. King Richard II and his government sheltered in the Tower of London. In the end, the rebels were tricked into going home. Wat Tyler, their leader, was killed, and many men were punished. But by this time the feudal system was no longer working properly and by 1400 the serfs had become free men.

During the Peasants' Revolt manor houses were burnt to the ground.

THE END OF SERFDOM

Slowly life in the Middle Ages changed. The lords of the manor found that serfs were poor workers. They were not paid for the work they did for their lords so they didn't do it carefully.

More and more lords found it better to pay their farm workers. Paid soldiers fought better than serfs, too. Serfdom, the system of landlords and serfs, gradually died out.

Men became either farmers of their own land, or labourers. The huge open fields were broken up into farms. By the end of the Middle Ages, some parts of the English countryside looked quite like they do today.

By 1400, the feudal system was coming to an end.

GLOSSARY

Ale   A kind of beer.
Baron   An important lord.
Chaff   The outside skin of corn.
Estate   A large amount of land owned by a person.
Harrow   A large rake used on farms.
Holy Day   The day on which a religious festival, like Christmas, falls.
Leech   A small creature that bites animals and drinks their blood.
Medieval   Something from the Middle Ages.

Middle Ages   The period in history between about AD 1000 and AD 1500.
Plague   A very serious outbreak of disease.
Population   The number of people living in a place.
Sickle   A long, curved knife used for cutting grass or cereal crops.
Spit   A metal spike on which meat is cooked over a fire.

MORE BOOKS TO READ

Michael Hobbs, *One Day in Medieval England* (Tyndall 1974).

Ray Mitchell and Geoffrey Middleton, *Norman and Medieval Britain* (Longman 1981).

Norman Scarfe, *Focus on History: Norman England* (Longman 1968).

Donald J. Sobl, *The First Book of Medieval Britain* (Franklin Watts 1970).

R. J. Unstead, *Living in a Medieval Village* (A & C Black 1971).

INDEX

Ale 19
Ale houses 26
Archery 27

Bear baiting 27
Black Death 20-21, 24
Books 23

Children 11, 14
Churches 6, 24-25
Clothing 4, 16-17
Common land 7
Cooking 8-9, 19
Cruck houses 8

Demesne 14

Edward II, King 27

Farming 12, 13, 14, 15
Festivals 27
Feudal system 5, 29, 30
Food and drink 4, 18-19,
 20
Football 27
Funerals 11

Harvest time 12, 18-19
Health 20-21
Holidays 26-27
Home life 8-9, 15
Hood, Robin 29
Houses and homes 8-9

Kings 5, 22
Kirtles 16, 17

Language 22-23
Latin 25
Lords of the manor 5, 6,
 7, 14

Marriage 10-11
Medicine 20, 21
Mills 6, 7, 14

Peasants' Revolt 29
Piers the Plowman 22
Pottage 19

Rebellion 25, 28-29
Religion 24-25
Richard II, King 29

Sport 27

Tyler, Wat 29
Typhoid 20

Villages 6-7

War 24, 28
Working life 4, 12, 13,
 14-15

Picture acknowledgements

The pictures in this book were supplied by the following: Janet and Colin Bord 25; BPCC/ Aldus Archives 12 (Bodleian), 14 (British Museum), 15 top (British Museum); E.T. Archive 13 (Osterreichische Nationalbib); Sheridan Photo Library 17 (bottom), 19 (bottom). The remaining pictures belong to the Wayland Picture Library.